UNLOCK

Vol.III

Jazz Etudes

For **C** instruments

JAZZ SWING
JAZZ BE-BOP
JAZZ FUSION
ODDTIME SIGNATURES
FUNK JAZZ
THREE TONIC SYSTEM
CONTEMPORARY
BALLADS

by
Sarpay Özçağatay

Unlock your musical identity

INTRODUCTION

Unlock VOL. III Jazz Etudes are designed to provide detailed aspects for players to improve their musicality, technical agility, articulations, dynamics, rhythmic studies and sight-reading skills. There are 12 etudes based on swing, bebop, contemporary, funk, ballad, jazz waltz and odd-time signature styles. Each etude focuses on different techniques for enhancing the players' understanding of the note-chord relationship along with all of the other skills listed above.

When working on these etudes, you should practice them slowly in the beginning and gradually raise the tempo as you become more comfortable with the etudes. Following this guideline will help you to retain what you're learning, depending your understanding of the etudes in the process.

In addition to playing through the etudes, it is also recommended that you do a harmonic analysis of each etude to understand the jazz approaches used in each piece.

Good luck with your studies,

All the best

Sarpay Özçağatay

TABLE of CONTENTS

Nº 1

This particular etude is composed and designed to play slurred notes continuously even, weather it is intervallic or linear phrases. The tempo mark is given between 160-180. For the first time, beginning with a slower tempo would provide you a better vision in terms of understanding the written music.

Breathing marks are not indicated during the piece, therefore players' breathing skills varies. It is always good to remember that when breathing, make sure that you prevent breaking phrases or even 8th note feeling.

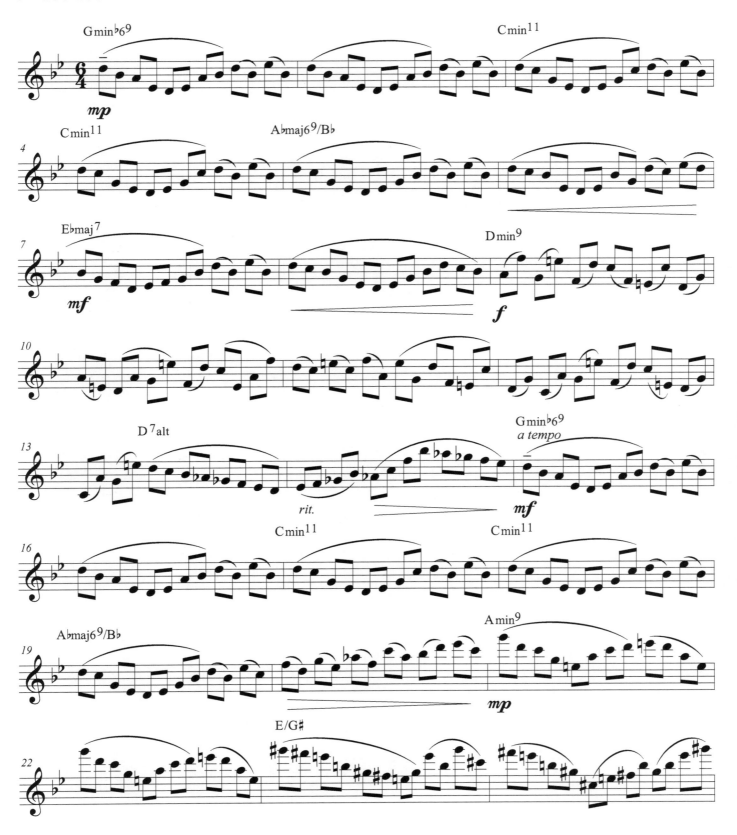

No 2

This through composed 9/8 time signature etude is designed to enhance familiarity with odd time signatures. 9/8 time signatures are very popular in Turkish, Balkan and Middle Eastern music.

Tempo mark is set to 260 for 8th notes. Beginning your studies at slower tempos will allow you to understand [and feel the] rhythmic divisions.

Gradually raising the tempo to 260 is recommended.

Nº 3

This etude focuses on intervallic studies, single or double-tonguing (for wind instruments) over F blues chord changes. As well as tonguing, players can also choose to play this etude slurred or their own articulation setting.

Tempo is set to 100-120, cut time.

Gradually raising your tempo to maximum will allow you to improve your technical agility.

$\half$ = 100-120 (even 8th)

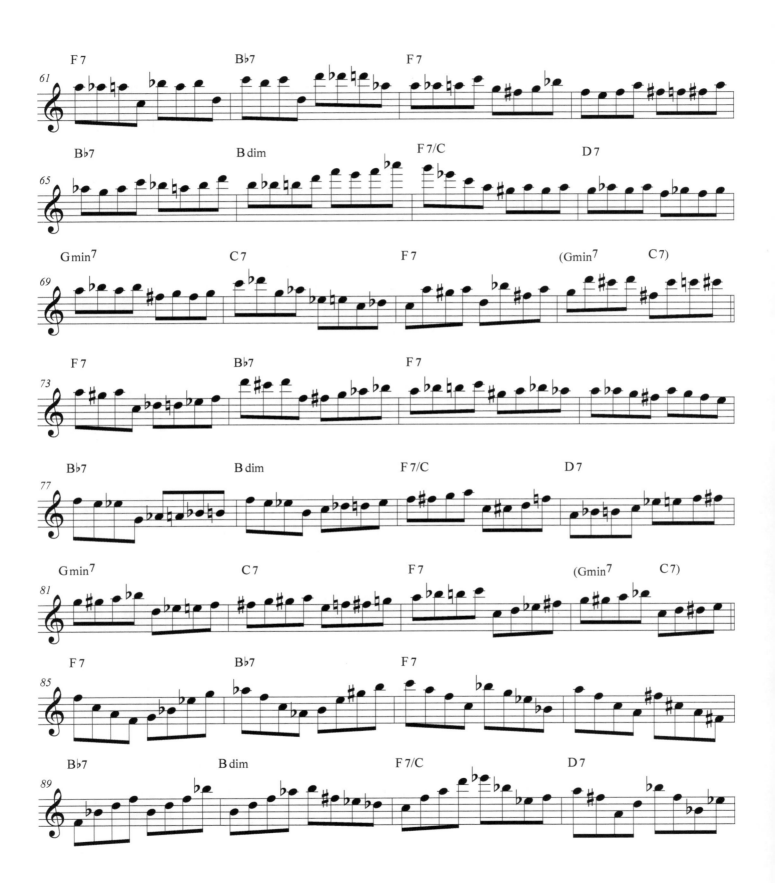

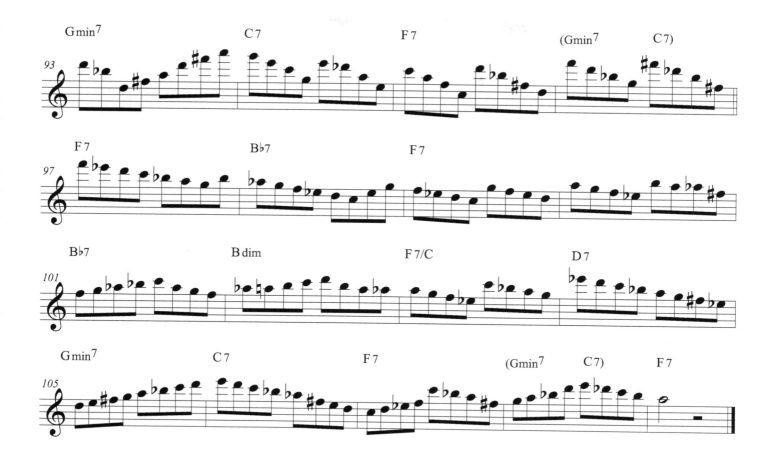

n⁰ 4

This Etude is designed to study three tonic system chord progressions over a swing feeling. John Coltrane composed the first and some of the most well known compositions using the three tonic system.

nº 5

Playing and improvising over ballads is a fundamental skill set that's necessary for becoming a better musician. This etude is created to provide you with some musical ideas that can be played over ballads.

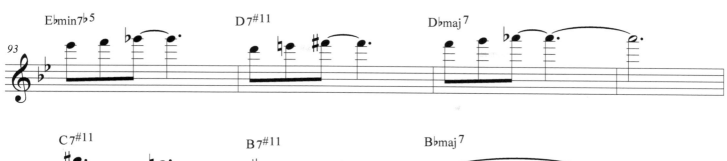

rit.

nº 6

This medium up-tempo swing etude is designed to work on your swing feeling within the indicated articulations. Practicing it at slower tempos and gradually speeding up is recommended.

nº 7

One of the most known chord progressions is Rhythm Changes. This etude is based on this progression, and it focuses on the swing feel and using be-bop language. Beginning your studies at a slower tempo is recommended.

n° 8

Minor blues for is one of the most popular music forms in jazz. This etude is created over the C minor blues form. There are a few techniques applied during the piece including pentatonic and "outside" approaches.

Nº 9

This composition is created in a 5/8 time signature. This unusual odd-time signature is mostly seen in Turkish, Middle Eastern and Balkan music cultures.

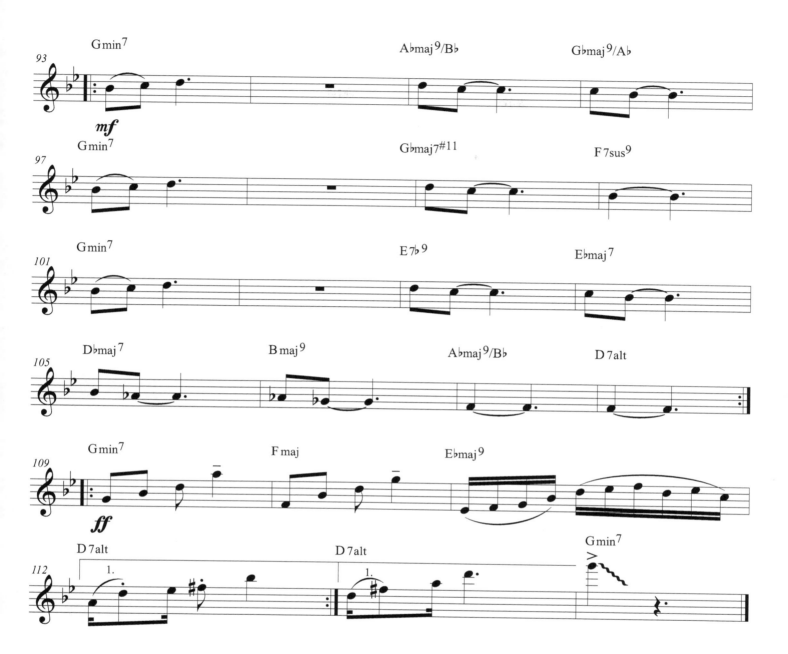

nº 10

This etude is designed and composed on chromatics. Chromatic playing is a fundamental technique for any instrumentalist. Single or double tonguing playing is recommended to study this etude.

nº 11

This etude is based on triplet studies. Playing even triplets and using them efficiently will bring you fascinating musical results. Practicing this etude slowly and detailed will allow your technical agility to grow to higher levels.

n⁰ 12

In one of the previous etudes, it was noted that playing over ballads are essential to become a better musician. This through composed composition over a chord changes is going to provide you with some more ideas to develop your ballad playing skills.

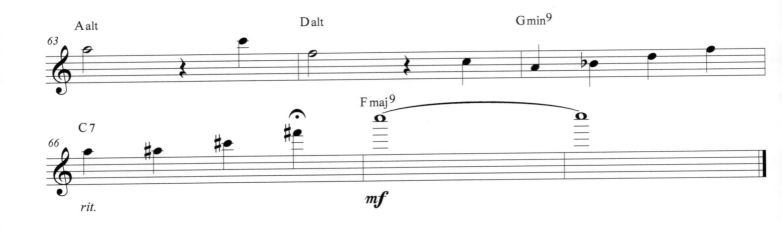

WORKSHEET